E S S E N T I A L F I N A N C E

DIVORCE AND FINANCES

STEPHANIE I. BLUM, ESQ.
AND
MARC ROBINSON

DORLING KINDERSLEY

London • New York • Sydney • Delhi • Paris • Munich • Johannesburg

A DORLING KINDERSLEY BOOK

Editors Stephanie Rubenstein
Design and Layout Jill Dupont
Photography Anthony Nex
Project Editor Crystal A. Coble
Project Art Editor Mandy Earey
DTP Designer Jill Bunyan
Photo Research Mark Dennis, Sam Ruston
Indexing Rachel Rice
Editorial Director LaVonne Carlson
Design Director Tina Vaughan
Publisher Sean Moore

First American Edition, 2000
24681097531

Published in the United States by
Dorling Kindersley Publishing, Inc.
95 Madison Avenue,
New York, New York 10016
See our complete catalog at
www.dk.com

Packaged by Top Down Productions
Copyright © 2000
Dorling Kindersley Publishing, Inc.
Text copyright © 2000 Marc Robinson

Dorling Kindersley Publishing, Inc. offers special
discounts for bulk purchases for sales promotions or
premiums. Specific, large quantity needs can be met
with special editions, including personalized covers,
excerpts of existing guides, and corporate imprints.
For more information, contact Special Markets Dept.,
Dorling Kindersley Publishing, Inc., 95 Madison Ave.,
NY, NY 10016; Fax: (800) 600-9098

Library of Congress Cataloging-in-Publication Data
Robinson, Marc, 1955-
Divorce and finances / Marc Robinson, Stephanie Blum.
p. cm. – (Essential finance)
Includes index.
ISBN 0-7894-6319-9
1. Divorced people–Finance, Personal. I. Blum, Stephanie II.
Title. III. Series
HG179 .R5475 2000
332.024'0653–dc21   00-031834

Reproduced by Colourscan, Singapore
Printed by Wing King Tong, Hong Kong

CONTENTS

INTRODUCTION

The financial consequences of divorce can often be as devastating as its emotional impact. Negotiating against someone with whom you once planned to spend the rest of your life can make this major life transition much more difficult. *Divorce and Finances* can help people cope with this potentially overwhelming task, particularly spouses who have had the least amount of involvement in financial planning and money management. The book is aimed at helping you understand your unique situation and become aware of some general guidelines involved in a divorce (that can vary immensely from state to state). It's also intended to help you measure your options against potential outcomes, select the appropriate professionals to help you, and make intelligent decisions to keep you financially sound as you move through and beyond divorce.

GETTING AN OVERVIEW

Money issues are also life issues. When you decide to divorce,
every aspect of your financial life becomes involved in
the separation between you and your soon-to-be ex-spouse.

SPLITTING ONE HOUSEHOLD INTO TWO

The overall issue is how to take the resources you've used to run one home and divide them to run two. There's no escaping this fact: Dividing everything ultimately leaves less for two single people than what was available to a married couple.

DIVIDE EVERYTHING

Splitting your resources can have profound implications for you and your ex-spouse's standard of living. The outcome will affect many parts of your life including where you live, where you work, what you do, and what you can afford to do. When you file for divorce the financial considerations focus around two main areas: property and support.

PROPERTY

Assets. Any assets accumulated during the marriage must be divided. First, you both have to make a list and agree about what property was acquired during the marriage. Then, you must either divide the items between the two of you or sell them and allocate the proceeds. Assets brought by one spouse to the marriage typically remain that spouse's separate property and aren't part of the property division.

Debts. Like the assets, debts accumulated during marriage must be divided, paid off, **or jointly assumed.**

 It's illegal for either spouse to hide assets in order to shield them from property division.

SUPPORT

You will need to work out who will pay for various expenses. Both of you may try to maintain a separate lifestyle as close as possible to what you had together. If, for example, you decide to keep your home, will spousal support be enough to cover the mortgage or rent? Also, what will child expenses cost and how much will each of you contribute to pay for them? Spousal support (alimony) and child support are designed to pay for living expenses. Your financial situation may require setting priorities and give up certain aspects of your previous lifestyle.

GOVERNING LAW

If you end up in court, a judge will typically have discretion to make subjective decisions as long as they abide by the laws of your state. Therefore, during settlement negotiations, it's wise to keep in mind the possible results of failing to settle and going to court instead.

EQUITABLE DISTRIBUTION

Most states are governed by the laws of equitable distribution. Everything accumulated during marriage is divided equitably (fairly) based on the needs of each spouse. A judge will typically take a subjective look at what seems a fair (equitable) standard of living for both parties after the marriage, based on the circumstances during marriage.

Some criteria used in dividing property and determining support may include:
- Length of the marriage;
- Each person's age and health;
- Each person's ability to earn an income;
- Childcare after the divorce and whether raising children during the marriage may affect one person's ability to earn income after the divorce;
- Whether one person was wasteful or negligent in using marital property during the marriage;
- In some cases, physical abuse or adultery.

COMMUNITY PROPERTY

In general, if you're in a state governed by community property laws, the starting point will be:
- To equally divide all the property accumulated during the marriage;
- To confirm to each party any property determined to be separate property.

In any settlement negotiations, you're free to work out any other arrangement you wish, as long as it doesn't violate your state's laws.

COMMUNITY ▲ PROPERTY
The states in green are governed by the laws of community property.

2 The laws governing divorce vary greatly from state to state. Check with your attorney.

SEPARATE PROPERTY

Issues of separate property can be a hotly disputed aspect of the proceedings. Assets that you or your spouse owned before you were married are generally considered to be separate (non-marital) property. Upon divorce, these assets aren't split; they're awarded to the spouse who first acquired those assets.

There are tests to determine whether or not certain property is separate. For example, did one spouse keep the property s/he owned before the marriage in his or her own name without ever commingling it with jointly owned property during the marriage? These are typical questions regarding cash: Was it kept in a separate account? Was it added to a joint account or was joint money added to it in the separate account?

Traced property. If a spouse can trace a contribution of his/her separate money to a down payment for, or improvements to, jointly owned property, s/he may have a claim for repayment.

Inheritances and gifts. These may be considered separate property. It's helpful to have written proof of the giver's intentions.

Debts. The debts owed by one person before marriage will probably be considered that person's sole responsibility to repay (see pg 46 for more on debt).

NO SMOKING?

At least two studies indicate that smoking may be a predictor of divorce (not a cause). In 1997, a long-term study by the Institute for Social Research at the University of Michigan concluded that smokers have a higher rate of divorce. A second study, by Eric and William Doherty, also determined that smoking increases the risk of divorce. They found that those who smoke have characteristics and life experiences that make them more divorce-prone than nonsmokers. Race, age, gender, and social and economic status were irrelevent. You might also keep in mind that creating second-hand smoke for children could lead to reduced custody or restrictions on smoking around children.

DOES FAULT MATTER?

In some states, the court can consider a spouse's fault in causing the divorce when deciding how to distribute property and decide support. In a no-fault divorce, the court won't look at issues of fault when making its determination.

THREE KEY DATES

There are three landmark dates in any divorce proceeding. Your rights and the arguments you may make to defend those rights could be greatly affected by the determination of these important dates.

DATE OF MARRIAGE

Your wedding date generally is regarded as the date that your marriage began. It may be possible, however, to have rights begin before that date in cases when people have lived together for many years. Property acquired during a marriage by either spouse individually, or by both spouses, tends to be considered marital property.

DATE OF SEPARATION

The date of separation can have a significant impact on who receives what. In some states, although not all, everything acquired, earned, or borrowed after this date may be separate property.

How the date of separation is determined varies from state to state, and may even vary from judge to judge. For example, it could be when one spouse moves out, or it could be the date you intended to live apart if neither of you were physically able to move out. It may be the date the divorce papers are filed in court, or sometime thereafter. In general, the date of separation is considered to be when one spouse's actions evidence a complete and final break in the marital relationship.

3 In many states, the court can allow a woman to keep her married name after the divorce.

DATE OF DIVORCE

When the final divorce decree is filed and accepted by the court, the marriage is officially over. This is an important date in terms of being able to remarry and and being able to file taxes as under the *unmarried* or *single* status.

In addition, neither person is responsible for the other's debts incurred after a divorce is finalized and neither person shares in new asssets acquired, unless you entered into an agreement that says otherwise.

FINAL DIVORCE WITHOUT A FINAL AGREEMENT

Can you be divorced before you finalize an agreement? In many states the answer is "yes." The typical case is one in which one spouse wants to remarry before all the issues such as child custody and visitation, support, distribution of property, and payment of attorney fees are resolved. In states permitting this *bifurcation*, the court will handle the end of the marriage separately from the other issues. Separating the divorce from the divorce agreement allows the parties to remarry while providing them additional time to resolve the remaining issues. The court retains the ability to resolve all remaining issues at trial if the parties can't finalize an agreement themselves.

4 In some states, dating while separated may be considered an act of adultery.

ATTORNEYS AND ALTERNATIVES

Just as a marriage is a legally binding contract between two people, a divorce is, first and foremost, a business deal. No matter how emotional you may feel now, it's wise to keep that in mind.

5 A divorce lawyer may be the only attorney prepared to represent your interests fully.

HIRE AN ATTORNEY

If you think you have less experience than your spouse in financial, legal, or business issues, it may be wise to hire a lawyer to help you protect all of your interests, especially if you have children. You may even find that, despite agreeing not to hire a lawyer, your spouse arrives in court with an attorney. If so, you may **have the legal right to ask the judge for an adjournment so you can also hire an attorney.**

If you think you can't afford a lawyer, you may at least want to pay for an hour's consultation to gain an overview of your rights and obligations. Find a lawyer who is mindful of your goals. You may want to ask for recommendations from others who've been through divorce. **Lawyers and even therapists may also be able to make useful recommendations.**

INFLEXIBILITY COSTS MONEY

The more money you spend fighting (in other words, paying lawyers and other professionals), the less you will have to divide between you. The less you have to split, the less flexible you can be. The less flexible you are, the longer you can expect it to take to settle disputes. The longer it takes to settle disputes, the more you will spend on the fight. The result can be a vicious cycle.

HIRE A MEDIATOR

Mediators don't represent either spouse. They listen to both sides and try to help you reach an agreement both of you can accept. In many cases, both people still hire their own attorney to review the mediated settlement before signing the final agreement. Mediators are often hired to resolve issues of child custody, parenting, visitation, property division, spousal support, and child support.

Consider seeking advice from a lawyer before commiting to mediation.

DO IT YOURSELF

In rare instances—for example, if you're divorcing without animosity, don't have children, own a simple set of assets, and both earn comparable incomes—you may be able get by without professional assistance. Still, you will need access to the proper forms and an understanding of how to complete and file the forms yourselves. Be sure to divide all the debts, not just the assets.

Document it. It would be wise to document everything you do in case a problem arises later (such as a tax audit). Documentation may include statements from each other stating that nothing has been hidden from the other spouse. Even if the documents are determined not to be legally binding, they may help you clarify issues at a later date.

Be informed. It still makes sense to read this book and other resources on divorce so that you understand the issues.

Know when to seek help. If potentially complex issues are involved (e.g., spousal or child support, business ownership, or a retirement plan), you would be well advised to seek professional assistance.

WHO CAN HELP?

*Y*ou don't have to face your financial future on your own. Many
professionals and organizations can be of assistance.

BANK OFFICER

If you don't have an accountant or if s/he is
working for your spouse, consider visiting
the manager at your bank. Bank officers are
often willing to help, particularly when
clients are in need. Some bank officers may
even act as your private financial consultant
during this time when you can use all the
support you can get.

FINANCIAL PLANNER

If you have a financial planner, s/he will
be familiar with your financial situation
and will probably be in tune with
important issues such as the goals you've
set and the strategies you had planned on
using to get there.

ACCOUNTANT

Your accountant should be familiar with
your financial situation. S/he will be in a
good position to help you develop a plan
to get back on your feet.

APPRAISER

When there's a question about an
asset's value, an appraiser can reduce
the risk of under- or overestimating its
worth. The appraiser can provide a
written opinion of value based on
prescribed methods of valuation,
research, and report writing.

ESTATE PLANNER

A professional estate planner can
help you minimize taxes, shield
assets from potential creditors,
protect your privacy, maximize the
use of your assets, find ways to
increase your income, help with
managing your finances, and help
you find other qualified
professionals in other fields to
support your financial goals.

FORENSIC
ACCOUNTANTS

Forensic accountants, specialize in
divorce. They're typically hired to
determine current and future values
of assets where reasonable people
could disagree on the value. They're
also often hired to trace income
and assets to determine whether:

● Additional income is available to
  pay child or spousal support;
● Assets belong to either one or both
  of the spouses;
● Income or assets have been
  hidden from one spouse.

GOING AFTER "DEADBEATS"

In 1992, the federal government passed the Child Support Recovery Act. This law focuses on people who willfully fail to pay past-due support obligations to a child living in another state. A judge can set a fine and/or imprison offenders for up to six months (repeat offenders can be imprisoned for up to two years). Be aware of these qualifications:

● Your ex-spouse and child live in the same state. The law doesn't apply to you;
● A judge must determine the amount of child support due. For the law to apply, there must be a court order specifying the amount due;

● If the amount due is $5,000 or less, it must be more than a year late for the law to apply;
● If the amount due is more than $5,000, there's no minimum time period;
● The person's failure to pay must be "willful." If s/he can show that it's been difficult or impossible to pay, the law might not apply.

This law is gaining popularity and publicity as a national trend toward cracking down on deadbeat parents grows. Some experts are unsure, however, whether it will be a cost-efficient way for parents to collect child support.

HELPFUL WEBSITES

The Child Support Network. If you're owed court ordered child support, you may want to contact the Child Support Network. For a fee, they assist in locating missing parents and collecting and enforcing court ordered child support payments. There are several payment plans available.

ACF/Office of Child Support Enforcement. At this site, you can read basic facts related to child support at www.acf.dhhs.gov/programs/cse/fctdsc.htm.

Chats. If you want to chat with others like you, go to www.divorcesupport.com and click on "chat rooms."

Financial planners specializing in divorce. For a list of financial planners in all fifty states, visit the Smart Divorce site at www.smartdivorce.com/divorce1.htm.
The institute for Divorce Financial Planners at www.institutecdp.com.

PREPARING TO NEGOTIATE

Any good negotiator will tell you that good preparation is vital to achieving your goals. You can help yourself by knowing where you are now and where you want to be.

CREATING A BUDGET

*B*udgeting and saving are the two basic principles of personal financial management. Anyone who takes the time to create a budget during divorce will be in a much better position to negotiate.

ONE-TIME EXPENSES

If you're the one moving out, include in your budget the cash you will need for deposits on rent or a down payment to buy a new home. You may also need cash to restock household supplies or buy furniture, appliances, and other large items. If you shared a car, you may want to have an idea of how much a **down payment would be for a second car.**

Even if you're not moving out, it may be helpful to gauge moving costs so that you can judge how reasonable your spouse is being when requesting money for these items. **Furthermore, you may also have to restock** items that become your spouse's property.

RECURRING EXPENSES

Calculate daily living expenses, such as running the household, caring for kids, dry cleaning, gas for the car, pet food, and regular maintenance of your home.

INTERMITTENT EXPENSES

Nearly everyone has expenses that arise infrequently, possibly only once each year. Many people forget these items when budgeting. For example:

Car. There may be repairs, tires, annual registration tax, etc.

Healthcare. Medical visits (even for pets) may be scheduled or unscheduled. Consider eyewear, orthodontics, and other similar care.

Activities. Consider expenses, such as camp, art, and sports programs, for you as well as for your children.

> **6** If your financial situation is burdensome, consider contacting a reputable, national, non-profit debt counseling service.

EXPERT RECOMMENDATIONS FOR SAVING MONEY

Many experts recommend strategies to build savings. Remember that cutting costs is an instant way to save money. If possible, add those savings to the money you put away and invest.

- Be disciplined. Live within your means.
- Save at least ten percent of every paycheck. Consider yourself as one of your own creditors—pay yourself first.
- Use your credit cards less. If you have a card with a high interest rate, look at transferring the balance to a new card with a low rate (there are many low-rate offers on the Internet, for example).
- Monitor how often you eat out. For many people, this expense turns out to be considerably more than they realize.
- Consider term insurance instead of whole life. Often, the cash values in whole life policies aren't worth the extra expense.
- Consider raising the deductibles on your car insurance. However, be more cautious about raising the deductible on health insurance, because you're likely to need its benefits more often than car insurance.
- Invest in securities that will help you reach your goals (e.g., income-producing bonds, if you need income; growth stocks if you're saving for longer-term needs).

17

BUDGET WORKSHEET

Figuring out how much you will need to live on shouldn't be a guess. Take the time to list the expenses you're likely to face. Here's a head start. Add anything else you can think of to the list because it's important not to leave out anything.

HOUSING EXPENSES

Rent/Mortgage   _____
Property taxes   _____
Condominium charges   _____
Coop maintenance charges   _____
Pool   _____
Gardening   _____
Housekeeping   _____
Household repairs   _____
Unexpected repair reserves   _____
Painting   _____
Furniture, accessories, linens   _____
Cleaning supplies   _____

UTILITIES

Water charges   _____
Electricity   _____
Telephone   _____
Cable   _____
Appliances and upkeep   _____

TRANSPORTATION EXPENSES

Car payments   _____
Car repairs   _____
Fuel   _____
Public transportation   _____

PERSONAL EXPENSES

Food   _____
Clothing   _____
Laundry   _____
Dry cleaning   _____
Clothing   _____
Books   _____
Magazines   _____
Newspapers   _____
Cigarettes   _____
Gifts   _____
Hair   _____
Lunches at work   _____
Courses   _____
Career Training
Hobbies   _____

INSURANCE

Life   _____
Disability   _____
Auto   _____
Personal property   _____
Fire, theft, liability   _____

MEDICAL EXPENSES

Medical insurance   _____
Dental   _____
Optical   _____
Prescriptions   _____
Other medicines   _____

ENTERTAINMENT

Vacation and travel   _____
Movies   _____
VCR rentals   _____
Theater   _____

DINING OUT

Restaurants   _____
Parties/entertaining _____

MISCELLANEOUS

Credit card debt   _____
Other loans   _____

Church or temple dues   _____
Charitable contributions _____
Association dues   _____

INCOME TAXES

Federal   _____
State   _____
Local (if any)   _____

CHILDREN

School tuition   _____
Summer camp   _____
Babysitter/childcare _____
Allowance   _____
School transportation
Child support   _____
Lessons   _____
Sporting goods   _____

OTHERS
(fill in with your own entries)

_____ _____
_____ _____
_____ _____
_____ _____

TOTAL   _____

COLLECTING RECORDS

D*ivorce negotiations often come down to having a clear, full picture of your financial status as a married couple, and to proving the arguments you decide to make.*

THREE MAIN TASKS

Copy. Make copies of all financial records, including wills, trusts, and the last few years of tax returns.

Record. Write down the names, addresses, account numbers, and any passwords of all bank, brokerage, insurance, credit card accounts, company retirement plans, etc. Store them in a safe place separate from your photocopies.

Visit. Check to see what's in your safe deposit box and write down the contents. You may want to take pictures, as well.

INCOME

Review your income from the past years (some experts recommend going back at least five years). This can be vital to negotiating support amounts and for discovering any money that may have been hidden from you.

Pay. Look at recent pay stubs, if available, and make copies. Try to get at least five stubs.

Statements. Collect at least several years' worth of bank statements to be able to document when and where all income was deposited (or that some income was not deposited). Credit card statements are also helpful.

Other. If you or your spouse received income from royalties, securities, rentals, bonuses, or other sources, you should document them.

CREDIT CARD RECORDS

Credit card receipts can help determine the type of lifestyle each person had during the marriage. Records showing a long pattern of spending indicate a consistent lifestyle. Records showing only recent spending indicate a change.

7 Keeping an organized filing system will save your accountant or attorney time, which will end up saving you money.

ASSETS

Cars. See that your car is in good working order. For all cars, look at the registration to see if it's owned jointly or just by you or your spouse. Review car insurance for who's name is on the policy (joint or single).

Insurance. Review all insurance policies relating to your home, the furnishings in the home, and personal belongings of value. If any items were individually appraised, detail them in your records along with the financial account information. Include photocopies of all appraisals (such as for your home and valuables).

Real estate. Review documents relating to any real estate you may own. List who owns it, when it was purchased (e.g., before or after marriage), the purchase price, any taxes owed, any liens against the property, and any income derived from it (including when the income is received).

Make copies of all:

- Deeds;
- Mortgages or other loan notes;
- Closing statements and contracts;
- Tax records;
- Appraisals.

OTHER DOCUMENTS

Life insurance. The policy will help understand how you or your spouse will be protected if one of you dies.

Pre- and post-nuptial. A pre- or post-nuptial agreement can have a significant impact on negotiations.

Passports. These may show times when your spouse left the country and could possibly have deposited assets elsewhere.

Powers of attorney. A power of attorney is a document that grants someone else the power to act on behalf of you or your spouse. For example, there may be a document that permits one spouse or even a third person to withdraw money from an account.

Business documents. If you and/or your spouse own a corporation or are part of a partnership, the documents that formed those entities can help determine present and future values of marital assets. Also look for profit and loss statements (P&Ls), balance sheets, or similar documents.

8 Take note who has actual possession of all assets and where the assets are physically located.

REVIEWING CREDIT

A credit report is a factual account of your borrowing and paying habits. It's important to order a copy to verify that what's being reported about you is current and correct. What's more, the report could alert you to activity by your spouse that could affect your own credit standing.

CHECK YOUR CREDIT STANDING

Credit history is one of the most common trouble spots for people after divorce because any activity on a joint account is the responsibility of both spouses. Many spouses, for example, do some "last minute" shopping with their joint credit cards before announcing a separation. Any failure to repay according to schedule becomes a joint failure to pay and is likely to end up on your individual credit report.

Check the statements of every joint account carefully. You can also call the toll-free number on the card and ask for a rundown of recent purchases. Then, either close the account or change the account to individual status.

NEED HELP?

You can contact a consumer organization, such as Genus Credit Management (www.genus2.org) or the National Foundation for Consumer Credit (www.nfcc.org).

> **9** People who don't have accounts in their name may have more difficulty getting credit on their own.

ORDER A REPORT

You're legally entitled to see your credit report as often as you wish, and to know how certain items got there. Many people order their reports before they apply for a loan. This gives them the opportunity to find mistakes or problems and to make an attempt to resolve them before a lender sees the report.

In most states, you're charged a small fee (around $8) to receive a copy of your report. You may contact a credit bureau directly (for example, see the list in the box below). There are also many websites that offer services to purchase your credit report.

WHO TO CONTACT

Thousands of local bureaus are located across the country. They're all connected to at least one of three national credit networks that collect the data. You may contact them at:
Experian: 888-397-3742
(www.experian.com)
Equifax: 800-997-2493
(www.equifax.com)
Trans Union: 800-888-4213
(www.transunion.com)

THINGS TO KNOW

Disputed information. Errors are inevitable. Have the credit bureau check anything you think is wrong or requires further explanation. Send your request in writing. Within approximately 30 days, the bureau should verify the information and send you the results. If you still dispute the report, you may include a written statement of 100 words or less in your credit file.

If credit is denied. You're entitled to a written explanation from the lender if you're denied credit. If the denial is based on your credit report, you're entitled to a free copy from the credit bureau, as long as you request it within 60 days.

Communicate. Stay in touch with creditors to minimize the effect of any negative activity that has occurred (or that you think might occur). With good communication, many creditors will try to work with you—for example by not reporting a late payment to the credit bureaus to create the least possible damage.

COMMON ERRORS

There are some common errors you may find in your credit report. They include:
- Confusing you with someone else who has the same name or a similar Social Security number;
- Failing to remove negative data after the issue is resolved;
- Failing to incorporate your comments into the file.

HOW TO READ A CREDIT REPORT

T*he information on these two pages gives you a head start toward understanding your credit report. Here's what you will find on most reports.*

NEGATIVE ITEMS ON YOUR REPORT

There are several ways you can deal with negative items on your credit report.

● Pay off any balances and ask the creditor to update your records;

● Wait for the information to be taken off your report;

● Write an explanation of the debt and ask the credit bureau to add it to your report. This can be effective when dealing with debts that are the result of economic hardship or unemployment. The negative item will not be removed, but future creditors may take your explanation into consideration.

---

10 Reports from different bureaus may look different but the kind of information on them should be much the same.

Company Name
This shows who issued the loan.

Account Number and Whose Account
This shows how you're responsible for the account.

Personal Identification Information

Mary Smith
555 Main St.
Town, State 99999

Credit Account Information

Company Name	Account Number and Whose Account
1st Nationwide Mortgage	Individual Account
Real estate mortgage Conventional mortgage	
American Express	
Credit card	Individual Account
Citibank - VISA	Individual Account
Countrywide	Joint Account
Real estate mortgage	
Express	Individual Account
Charge	
First USA Bank	

Additional Information
This shows the type of loan. Any other information the lender feels is necessary is listed under the company name.

Date Opened
This shows when your loan account was opened.

Type of Account and Status
This shows the type of account and the payment status.

Last Activity
This shows the last time this acccount was used.

High Credit
This shows the highest amount you owed since the account was opened.

Call this number with questions -
Request Reference:
Report Date: 12 November 1999

CREDIT PROFILE

Social Security Number:
Date of Birth:

Terms
This shows the payment amount and/or the length of the loan.

Items as of Balance
This is the remaining amount due on the loan at the time the report was sent.

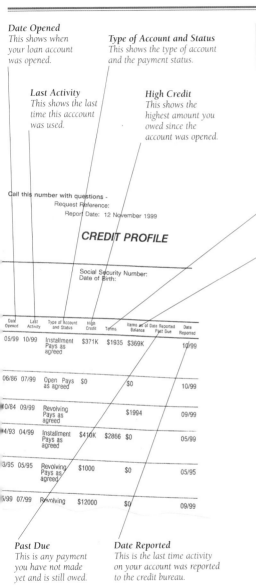

Date Opened	Last Activity	Type of Account and Status	High Credit	Terms	Items as of Balance	Date Reported Past Due	Date Reported
05/99	10/99	Installment Pays as agreed	$371K	$1935	$369K		10/99
06/86	07/99	Open Pays as agreed	$0		$0		10/99
0/84	09/99	Revolving Pays as agreed			$1994		09/99
4/93	04/99	Installment Pays as agreed	$410K	$2866	$0		05/99
3/95	05/95	Revolving Pays as agreed	$1000		$0		05/95
5/99	07/99	Revolving	$12000		$0		09/99

Past Due
This is any payment you have not made yet and is still owed.

Date Reported
This is the last time activity on your account was reported to the credit bureau.

POSITIVE AND NEGATIVE DON'T BALANCE

A large amount of positive credit doesn't usually outweigh items of negative credit. Any negative credit is an obstacle in the way of a lender's "yes" to your request.

THINGS TO KNOW

Joint credit is based on the assets, income, and credit history of both people who apply. Married couples often apply for joint credit. You may get more credit this way, but you will both be responsible for the debt—even if you get divorced.

SEPARATING JOINT ACCOUNTS

As soon as possible after separating, you may want to manage all of your finances through separate accounts. The easier it is to show separate money, the fewer conflicts there may be over who has rights to that money.

BANK ACCOUNTS

Freezing. It's fairly common for one spouse to try to empty a bank account either upon learning of the divorce or before telling the other spouse that s/he wants a divorce. It may be possible for you to request your bank to either freeze the money in your accounts or require that both spouses sign withdrawal slips over a certain amount. Check with your bank officer. Here are two possible ways to deal with joint bank accounts.

Escrow account. An escrow account is a special type of account that an officer of the bank is assigned to monitor. The officer must receive written authorization from both parties before any transaction involving the account can occur.

Dividing the money. In a more amicable situation, you might decide to each take half of the money and deposit it into new, separate accounts.

If you don't have joint bank accounts, your spouse may use all of the money and leave you to negotiate its return. Remember the saying, "possession is nine-tenths of the law?"

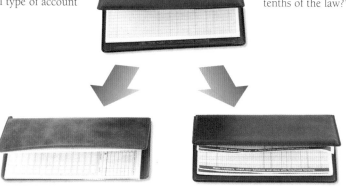

JOINT CREDIT CARDS

If you use a joint credit card for purchases you will be jointly obligated to repay the debts. What's more, creditors aren't bound by any divorce resolution. That's why it's important to consider closing joint accounts and opening separate accounts even if you have no credit history and must start out with a secured credit card.

The process. To close joint accounts, notify each creditor in writing of the divorce. Ask to close the account and cancel the cards. If the account can't be closed until fully repaid, ask for it to be placed on inactive status and closed once the balance is paid in full. Ask for the most recent statement so you can see the most up-to-date information. If you send the letters by certified mail you will have proof of receipt by the creditors. If you don't get satisfaction from the person on the phone, ask to speak to a supervisor.

Word of caution. If you cancel a card, you may leave your ex-spouse without adequate spending capability. Since that may anger him (her), negotiations could become more difficult.

 Joint responsibility for debts incurred during your marriage will continue even after you're divorced.

BROKERAGE ACCOUNTS

Consider any brokerage accounts when deciding whether to create separate accounts. Act quickly. If selling and withdrawing money requires only one spouse's signature, you may end up without the savings you thought you once had, and instead find yourself in the middle of a negotiation to get back your share of the funds.

SAFE DEPOSIT BOX

A safe deposit box can easily be emptied without your knowledge. Whoever gets there first has the upper hand. You probably have little chance of recovering the items that were in a safe deposit box, which can have emotional as well as financial consequences, since many people keep sentimental items in safe deposit boxes. You may have some recourse if you have taken inventory of the box and photographs of everything inside. You will have a little more credibility if you have an officer of the bank sign your inventory. It may be possible to obtain a restraining order from the court to keep your spouse from removing anything until a final settlement is reached or a new court order is issued.

DIVIDING ASSETS AND DEBTS

One of the most important, and potentially volatile, aspects of a divorce involves identifying all of the assets and debts, assigning value to each one, and determining how they will be divided.

ASSETS AND DEBTS ACQUIRED PRE-MARRIAGE

One of the first steps is to determine what assets and debt are separately owned by each spouse and what assets and debts remain open to negotiation.

SEPARATE PROPERTY

The list of assets to be divided won't include any assets and debts that are determined to be the separate property of one spouse. For example, in some states, inheritances and gifts clearly made to one spouse become that spouse's separate property. In addition, property brought by one spouse to the marriage may be separate property. Likewise, the earnings from that property may also be considered separate property.

WHEN PROPERTY IS VALUED

Typically, the valuation of assets is performed as close as possible to the trial date (if you have one). Between the date of separation and the date of trial, an asset's value can fluctuate, and that change can have an impact on the value of each spouse's total assets. This scenario is particularly true with stocks and other securities that fluctuate on a daily basis.

COMMINGLED ACCOUNTS

Money that was once separate but has been placed in a joint account or commingled in some other way may still end up being separate property if the money can be traced back to its original source.

 12 A court may nullify a premarital agreement if it's written in a way that would likely promote a divorce.

FORMAL AGREEMENTS

Couples can enter into two types of written, signed agreements outlining the division of property and other rights in the event of divorce. Typically, to be valid, the agreement must be voluntarily entered into and be made with fair and reasonable disclosure of property and financial obligations.

Premarital agreements. This agreement is made before the marriage. If done properly, a premarital agreement will be presumed valid.

Postmarital agreements. Couples may also enter into an agreement after they're married. Typically, this is not as easy to enforce as a properly prepared premarital agreement.

The reasoning behind the differences in the enforceability of pre- and postmarital agreements lies in the following logic: Married people have a fiduciary duty to each other, but unmarried people don't have a fiduciary duty to each other even if they're contemplating marriage.

THE HOME

A home is typically one of the largest family assets, or at least one of the largest issues, in divorce. The emotions of having to leave your home or possibly having to sell it to make ends meet can make difficult financial issues even more difficult to handle.

IF YOU'RE STAYING

Many divorcees try to keep their home, particularly if children are involved. Unless otherwise agreed, if you're staying in the home, you will be responsible for expenses such as rent or mortgage, repairs, and maintenance. It's possible to negotiate an arrangement where the one living in the home covers all reasonable and necessary expenses up to a certain dollar amount but beyond that, expenses are either split or covered by the other spouse entirely.

13 Moving out of your home may affect your future rights. Consult an attorney to better understand your own situation.

IF YOU'RE MOVING OUT

The spouse moving out may have issues concerning liability for the home. If you're an owner, a mortgage lender probably won't allow your name to be taken off the loan. In either case, the rationale is that there would be one less person to go after if there is a need to collect an overdue payment.

If you own the home, you may be responsible for the:

● Mortgage;
● Taxes;
● Insurance;
● Any liens against the property placed by contractors or other workers who haven't been paid.

If you want to keep tabs on your liabilities, you may want duplicate copies of payment notices and monthly statements sent directly to you.

It may be wise for you to agree to cover at least a portion of certain expenses that might impact on the home's value. In this way, you will be protecting your interest by maintaining a well-kept home.

OTHER ISSUES TO CONSIDER

● If you're moving out, you may want to request a refinancing of the mortgage so that your name can be removed from the new loan.

● You may agree to sell your interest in the home to your ex-spouse instead of selling the home outright. Be aware, though, that once told of the transfer, the lender may insist that the loan be repaid in full if it has a "due on sale" clause in the loan agreement.

● In some states, it may be possible for the person remaining in the home to be charged the fair rental value for the amount of time s/he lived in the home between the separation and the final divorce. Alternatively, if you are the spouse making the mortgage payments, you may be entitled to a claim for reimbursement of the mortgage payments made after separation and before the final divorce.

● If you find yourselves in a stalemate about who will leave and who will remain in the home, you may lose the right to resolve the issue to the satisfaction of either party. The court may simply order you to sell the home and divide the proceeds.

SELLING THE HOME

If you own your home, it may be more valuable for the cash it can generate from a sale than as a residence. With two households to support, you may decide that the best course of action is to sell your home and divide the proceeds.

WHO OWNS THE HOME

Whose name is on the title may not be the ultimate controlling factor in determining who actually owns the home. For example, in community property states, one spouse may have owned the home prior to marriage and is the only name appearing on the title. If, however, both spouses made mortgage payments (for example, from income earned during the marriage) it may be determined that the other spouse has acquired an interest in the home, depending on your state's laws.

The percentage of joint ownership will likely be based in large part on how much of the loan principal was repaid with joint funds, and/or the value of any improvements.

WHO RECEIVES THE PROCEEDS

In community property states, if the home is jointly owned and you use separate property (e.g., your own money) to make repairs or improvements, you may be entitled to a reimbusement for that money, assuming you've kept good records and can trace the source of your payments to your separate money.

PROTECTING THE EQUITY

If both parties remain co-owners of the home, it may be wise to agree that neither one would have the ability to borrow money using the home as collateral without permission from the other. In this way, both parties can protect their interest in the home's value and maximize the equity in the home upon an eventual sale.

◀ TAX BREAKS
You may be able to deduct certain moving expenses on your income tax return if the move is related to starting work in a new location.

14 If one spouse buys out the other spouse's interest, the IRS won't consider it a sale for tax purposes.

WHO RECEIVES THE TAX BREAK

One spouse may remain in the house while the other moves out. Previously, when the house was sold, the spouse who moved out owed capital gains tax on his (her) share of the profit (because the home was no longer that spouse's main residence). The Taxpayer Relief Act of 1997 changed the law so that today:

- As long as you moved out in accordance with a legal divorce or separation agreement, both parties can claim a tax break.
- The maximum excluded gain is $250,000 for an individual or for a married person filing separately.
- If either ex-spouse is remarried or you're still filing as married, that person's share of gain could be excluded up to $500,000.

To receive the exclusion, you must have lived full-time in the home for at least two of the five years before the sale.

IF YOU AGREE TO SELL THE HOME

You may want to agree about:
- Who will be the listing broker;
- What the listing price will be;
- What the lowest selling price will be.

You may also want to agree that the person remaining in the home will cooperate with brokers and keep the home presentable at all times during the selling period.

SMALL BUSINESSES

You may not want to be partners with your ex-spouse after a divorce. After all, most people say that partnerships are like a marriage.

ENDING THE RELATIONSHIP

Dividing a business can be very complicated. Expert assistance is required to determine how much the business is worth, what liabilities it may face, and more. Here are some general ideas about dividing a business in divorce.

If one spouse owns the business. A court usually won't force a spouse to sell a business if it's the spouse's primary source of income. This becomes an even stronger argument if that income is also the primary means for paying spousal or child support.

If both spouses are owners. You both will have to decide whether to continue your working relationship despite ending the marital relationship. Typically, one spouse will buy out the other's portion of ownership. This could be structured in one of several ways:

- Make an all-cash payment. This keeps the deal simple;
- Pay cash in installments. Until the buyout is complete, the spouse who's selling could hold the business as security in case the buying spouse defaults on the payments;
- Trade the business ownership for another asset (such as a home)—or series of assets—of equal value to the business.

THINGS TO CONSIDER

Here's a partial list of questions to ask:

- How is ownership of the business held and what type of ownership is it (e.g., stock ownership, sole proprietorship, partnership)?
- Is there an opportunity for each spouse to receive separate businesses by splitting up the existing business?
- Is the business interest a part of the marital or community estate?
- What is the value of the business interest for purposes of a divorce?
- What income tax liabilities come with ownership of the business interest?
- What other property is there in the marital or community estate that could be used to offset the value of the business interest?

15 Consider whether you want children to retain interest in the business. If so, consult an estate planner.

DOCUMENTS TO COLLECT

Here is a list of of some of the documents you may need in valuing and dividing a jointly owned business:

- State and federal income tax returns for the past five years;
- Financial statements for the past five years;
- Interim financial statements since the last year-end statements;
- An inventory of assets and each asset's location and current market value;
- Appraisals of any assets;
- Any letters of intent or purchase offers that you have received during the past five years;
- Any buy-sell agreements or partnership agreements;
- Stock certificates;
- List of other shareholders and their number of shares;
- Schedule of accounts;
- General ledger for the past five years;
- Current accounts receivable;
- Current accounts payable;
- List of customers and the percentage each customer provides of your total sales;
- Any special purchasing agreements or service agreements with a vendor;
- Non-compete agreements;
- Notes payable to shareholders, partners, or owners;
- Notes receivable from shareholders, partners, or owners;
- Any trust or other estate planning documents containing information about how you acquired your ownership interest in the business;
- Any trust or other estate planning documents showing current ownership structure or future ownership structure;
- List of any loans or debts of the business that you or your spouse have personally guaranteed;
- List of any perquisites or benefits that the company provides for you, your spouse, and for your children or other family members and the cost to the company for providing the perquisite or benefit;
- Any business valuations that were done during the past 5 years.

VALUING A BUSINESS

The value of a jointly owned business can play a significant role in the overall division of property. Finding common ground on the value of the business and how to divide it is often one of the most contested—and expensive—aspects of divorce.

APPRAISED VALUE

There are a variety of standards an accountant or business appraiser might use to determine the value of a business. You might want to use your own accountant or consider hiring a valuation expert to appraise your business. Here are a few of the commonly used standards.

Fair market value. This is the most widely recognized method. In general terms, it's the cash or cash equivalent price at which a property would change hands between a willing buyer and willing seller, with both being adequately informed of all the facts surrounding the property.

Book value. Simply put, the term *book value* comes from the process of totaling the value of all assets and deducting the value of all debts as shown on the company books. Many experts believe this is not the best way to value a company for divorce purposes.

Liquidation value. Another standard involves looking at what the sales price would be if the company went out of business and all of its assets were sold. One test is based on an orderly liquidation sale when there's no rush. The other is based on a forced (or distress) sale when selling quickly is more important than getting the best price. You should expect that an orderly sale value will produce a higher price than a price received from a forced sale.

OTHER STANDARDS

An accountant reviewing your case might also use the following standards to value a business:

- Excess earnings method;
- Multiple of gross or net earnings (rules of thumb);
- Capitalization of earnings.

PROFESSIONAL GOODWILL

Some, if not most, states recognize goodwill as a component in determining the value of practices for doctors, lawyers, accountants and other personal service professionals. Ask your lawyer.

16 If your spouse won't cooperate and provide the books, ask for a court order.

FINANCIAL STATEMENT

This is the document produced each year to show the net worth of the business. In small businesses that are not public companies (they don't trade stock on a stock exchange) these statements may be prepared by the company or by an outside accountant.

Check the purpose. If the statement was prepared in anticipation of getting a bank loan, it may differ from statements prepared for tax purposes.

INTANGIBLES

Most businesses are affected by intangible factors that could alter their value. Some examples are goodwill, patents, and trademarks.

An accountant will apply one or more calculations to come up with a current value for those intangible valuations. These calculations can be complex. You can expect them to differ in results depending on whether your accountant or your spouse's accountant is doing the calculations.

TAPPING INTO RETIREMENT ASSETS

*A*ssets from retirement plans can be a significant portion of the marital property to be divided. If retirement savings are to be divided, try to avoid any 10% penalty tax for early withdrawal.

WHAT IS A RETIREMENT PLAN?

There are two main categories of retirement plans.

Defined benefit plans. In these plans, the amount of the benefit the plan participant (usually the employee) will receive at retirement is determined in advance. When most people mention a *pension plan*, they're talking about a defined benefit plan.

Defined contribution plans. In these plans, the plan participant determines in advance how much will be contributed to his/her retirement account. The amount of the benefit at retirement is, however, unknown. The amount of savings will depend on the success of the participant's investments. Employer sponsored plans such as 401(k)s, 403(b)s, Keoghs, and profit sharing plans are defined contribution plans.

There are many other types of plans, including retirement accounts for individuals, such as traditional IRAs. Keep in mind that each type of retirement plan has rules governing the withdrawal of funds. Check with a professional familiar with the rules.

▼ **TAPPING INTO ASSETS EARLY**
The 10% penalty doesn't **apply to retirement assets withdrawn before age 59 1/2 if withdrawn in "substantially equal amounts." There are many rules to follow, so consult with your tax advisor or** *attorney.*

17 Money transferred directly to a spouse (instead of directly to an IRA) is taxable in that year.

THE "AGE 55" EXCEPTION

Once you reach age 55, the IRS allows you to take withdrawals from a 401(k) without the 10% penalty, if you meet certain requirements. Ask your tax advisor.

WHAT IS THE VALUE?

The value of the account depends on issues such as the plan's vesting rights, and other plan-specific rules. Vesting refers to the amount of money in the account the employee would be entitled to keep if s/he left the company. In general, any money the employee contributes is automatically vested. Any money the employer contributes will become the employee's to keep based on the plan's vesting schedule. In individual plans, such as IRAs, all the money in the account is automatically the account **holder's to keep.**

SURVIVING SPOUSES

If an employee's spouse remarries before the QDRO is issued, the new spouse will be entitled to surviving spouse rights. Therefore, if you're the non-employee, it's wise to obtain a QDRO naming yourself as the surviving spouse before the marriage is dissolved.

AVOIDING TAXES

A Qualified Domestic Relations Order (QDRO) is a tool used to divide retirement plan assets between spouses to avoid tax consequences. It's also a legal document that gives an employer (or plan administrator) permission to transfer the employee's plan assets to the spouse.

401(k)s, pension plans, and other company-sponsored plans. A QDRO may be required in order to give the company benefits department permission to transfer money to a non-employee.

IRAs and other individual retirement accounts. A QDRO isn't required for spouses to transfer these assets without tax consequences. The spouse with the account makes a written request to the firm holding the account to transfer money directly into the other spouse's Rollover IRA, a type of IRA set up specifically to accept transferred (rolled over) assets.

INSURANCE

You need to think about health and life insurance. Where one policy was covering the family, there will now be a need for separate policies.

HEALTH INSURANCE

The costs of medical care can be astronomical. As a result, resolving medical insurance issues should be an important part of your financial planning in divorce.

In some states, the obligation of one spouse to pay the insurance for the other spouse ends upon divorce (not upon separation).

In contrast, the obligation to maintain insurance for the children usually continues until they are 18 or 19, depending on your state's laws. Typically, spouses negotiate how much each will contribute toward items such as:

- The cost of the policy;
- Unreimbursed medical, dental, and orthodonture expenses;
- Psychotherapy sessions.

SELF-PROTECTION

If your spouse has the healthcare plan, you will want to take steps to ensure that coverage is maintained for you during separation. For example you should:

- Have a copy of the current insurance ID card so you will know the policy number and the toll-free number in case of emergency;
- Ask for duplicate copies of notices from the insurer about premium payments and any policy changes;
- Be sure that your spouse cooperates in processing claims;
- Agree about who will pay the expenses that insurance doesn't cover, including deductibles.

In some states, it's illegal to change insurance coverage once you file for divorce. Automatic restraining orders go into effect in order to protect one spouse from potential punitive actions by the other spouse.

LIFE INSURANCE TO GUARANTEE SUPPORT PAYMENTS

If your ex-spouse is required to support you or your children, you may want to guarantee the support with a life insurance policy to cover payments should your ex-spouse die. In some states, the court can actually order the spouse paying support to buy life insurance. Ask to receive notices of premium payments and policy changes.

WHOLE LIFE POLICIES AS ASSETS

If you or your spouse have a whole life insurance policy, it may have a cash surrender value, meaning that you can receive cash if you end the policy before dying. The policy may also let you borrow against the cash value, making it a valuable asset in time of need.

TEMPORARY HEALTH INSURANCE

Your spouse may continue to provide health insurance for the children, but s/he can't provide coverage for you through the employer's group plan. This is because you're no longer a member of his or her family. If your spouse's employer has more than 20 employees, you may be able to receive termporary coverage under the COBRA laws.

COBRA laws require insurance companies to offer continued coverage to family members for up to 36 months after either the employee leaves work without other coverage or after a divorce. The coverage must be equivalent to the coverage available through the company plan. The insurance must also be offered at a fairly comparable price.

Talk to the insurer before the COBRA coverage expires about converting the policy to a plan of your own to see how much it will cost. If it seems too expensive, you will need time to find a more affordable plan to which you can switch.

18 Certain employers must provide COBRA coverage if they receive notice within 60 days after the divorce.

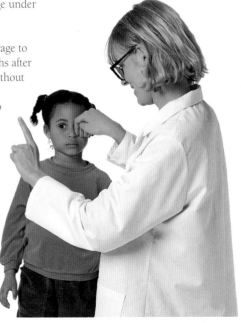

Hidden Assets

If someone has been planning a divorce for a while, and if that person is so inclined, he or she might devise numerous strategies for hiding money from a spouse and children. With the right legal help, however, wronged spouses can often come away with much of what is rightfully theirs.

ILLEGAL TRANSFERS

A devious spouse might try to reduce the amount of assets declared during divorce proceedings by wrongfully transferring assets or income to a friend or family member and then claim that s/he no longer has these assets. Your lawyer will then have to prove that an improper transfer was made. In these cases, you or your lawyer can hire an accountant, called a *forensic accountant*, who specializes in tracing assets and income, to help you get back what you deserve.

19 Question whether finding an asset might cost more than the value of the asset itself.

CONCEAL ASSETS AT YOUR OWN PERIL

Recently, a California woman won the state lottery, didn't tell her husband, then filed for divorce. All of the known assets were divided and the divorce was finalized. In 1999, the husband mistakenly received a notice in the mail from a company interested in paying his ex-wife a lump sum in exhange for the remaining lottery payments. Alerted, he sued, claiming that he was entitled under California law to half of the winning amount and that she had defrauded him. The court ruled in his favor—awarding him the *entire* amount of the winnings.

COMMON TRICKS

Here are some tricks you, your lawyer, or a forensic accountant will look for to see whether your spouse has discolosed all assets:

Secret bank accounts. Opening accounts without letting the other spouse know;

Checks to cash. Writing checks to "cash" and hoarding or stashing some of the money instead of spending it on family expenses;

Retirement funds. Having the employer make contributions to a retirement account without letting your spouse know that money is being put away for the benefit of both spouses;

Kickbacks. Overpaying vendors and having them "kickback" the overpayment in cash;

Cashing checks. Not depositing customer checks in the business account, and instead cashing them directly at the bank so they don't appear on the business statements;

Oversupplies. Ordering excess supplies for the business, returning them and asking the vendor to refund the amount to the spouse personally—who then cashes the refund check;

Phony vendors. Paying phony vendors and cashing the checks at the bank—the spouse may have an arrangement with the teller.

SOCIAL SECURITY BENEFITS

Many people may not be aware that Social Security benefits may be an asset of marriage. Here are the general rules for determining whether you or your spouse will one day receive benefits as a widowed ex-spouse.

WHO'S ENTITLED?

Federal law entitles anyone married for at least ten years to receive Social Security benefits based on the other spouse's earnings. The benefit is called a derivative benefit. It's half of your ex-spouse's benefits. To benefit, you must apply after you reach age 62 and you may not be remarried. Here are some key points:

- You don't have to address this issue in your divorce decree. It's effective automatically;

- You're entitled to begin collecting the benefits even if your ex-spouse keeps working;
- The amount of your benefit is based on your ex-spouse's entire earnings history, not just on his/her earnings during marriage;
  - The benefits you receive won't reduce your ex-spouse's benefits or the benefits of anyone in his/her family;
  - If your own earnings through retirement are higher than your ex-spouse's, your benefits will be based on your own earnings, not his/hers.

GOVERNMENT PENSIONS

A pension from a government job you held will reduce the amount of Social Security you receive. But a pension you receive from your ex-spouse's government job won't reduce your Social Security benefits.

GROWING POPULATION

According to the Social Security Adminisration, the population at or above age 65 (normal retirement age), will rise from 34 million in 1995 to 87 million in 2080—a more than 150 percent increase.

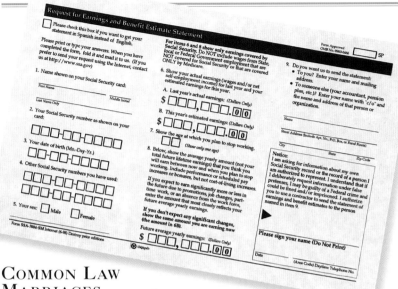

COMMON LAW MARRIAGES

Some states have statutes which recognize couples as married even though there was no formal ceremony. A divorcing person married by common law for over ten years may be entitled to Social Security benefits.

SOCIAL SECURITY▲ BENEFITS ESTIMATE

Anyone can order a Social Security Benefits Estimate based on their own situation. You can order it online from the Social Security Administration website at www.ssa.gov. There is also an option on the site to order it by mail.

DISABILITY BENEFITS

In Mathews v. de Castro, (1976), the Supreme Court ruled that a married woman under age 62 whose husband retires or becomes disabled may be paid monthly benefits if she has an entitled child in her care, but the benefits do not extend to a similarly situated divorced wife on the basis of her ex-husband's retirement or disability.

20 Generally, a non-working spouse can receive up to 50% of the Social Security benefit available to the working spouse.

DIVIDING DEBT

No less important than dividing assets is dividing the outstanding debts. The basic guidelines are similar to, but not the same, as asset division.

WHO'S RESPONSIBLE?

Two main factors determine who will be responsible for repaying a debt: when the debt was incurred, and who benefited from it. Neither one, however, is conclusive or automatic.

Debts during marriage. In some states, if a spouse incurred an expense for something that had no benefit for the other spouse (a hobby, for example), the debt may be considered that spouse's sole responsibility. In other states, such as some community property states, debts incurred during marriage are the equal responsibility of both spouses, even if only one spouse received a benefit from money spent.

Debts brought to marriage. In some states, debts incurred prior to marriage (separate, or non-marital debts) are considered the sole responsibility of the spouse who incurred it.

For family benefit. In some states, one test used is whether the debt was incured for the benefit of the family. Household items, health care, and family trips, for example, are typically considered for the family benefit.

21 Statistics reveal that 80 percent of people who divorce do so because of financial problems

WHO'S DEBT IS IT?

When debts are divided, each spouse takes responsibility for repaying debts assigned to them. Creditors, however, aren't bound by the terms of a divorce agreement or decree. They can demand payment from you, regardless of whether or not the debts were assigned to you. As protection, you may add a clause in your divorce agreement providing that if the party to whom the debt is assigned fails to repay it, the other party would be entitled to indemification.

THINGS TO KNOW

If your spouse filed fraudulent tax returns or hid money from you and the IRS, you can try to show that you had absolutely no knowledge or involvement and claim no liability under the Innocent Spouse Rule. If you think you are in a situation such as this, consult an accountant or attorney for assistance.

TO DO LIST

As soon as you know you are separating:

● Make a list of all current debts, especailly credit card. Analyze the interest rate of each loan and card. Create a written plan to start reducing or eliminating these debts.

● Close all credit card accounts that are either joint or "authorized-user" and open new separate accounts. Inform card issuers of accounts you're closing that you're separating. Request that the issuer state that you closed the account so it doesn't appear to be closed because of bad debt.

● Inform any other lenders that you have separated and that you don't want any changes in the loan to occur without your permission. Ask for current balances and the type of account.

● List when each loan began and the reason why you and/or your spouse received it. Include who has been making the payments, the monthly amount paid, and the amount currently owed to the lender.

WATCH YOUR CREDIT

Negative credit marks accumulated by one spouse may be transferred to the other's credit standing, often without that spouse's knowledge.

JOINT AND SEVERAL LIABILITY

If both spouses co-signed for a debt, or if a debt was incurred through a joint account, such as a joint credit card, both spouses will probably have joint and several liability for the debt. The term means that each spouse is individually responsible for the entire debt if that debt isn't repaid.

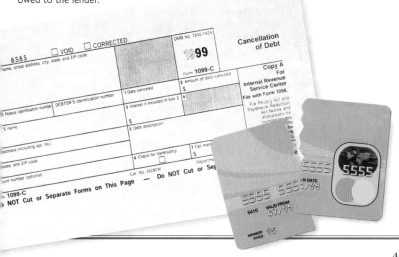

DETERMINING SUPPORT

Divorce usually involves determining how much one spouse will pay the other to help defray basic living expenses. There are two basic kinds of support: spousal support (alimony) and child support.

CHILD SUPPORT

Most states set guidelines for calculating child support. As with virtually everything else in divorce cases, it varies from state to state. There are also many exceptions and special considerations that apply. If you don't agree on your own, the court will apply the formulas of your state. It's impossible, therefore, to state any hard and fast rule about how much you should expect to pay or to receive.

COMPARATIVE INCOMES

The most important factor in determining support is how much income is available to both spouses. Typically, if the matter goes to trial or to a hearing, the court will look at the income each spouse has received during the previous 12 months and base the percentage of support on the total income of both spouses. Be aware, though, income can be defined broadly to include every possible source, whether salary, royalties, rent, dividends and interest, etc., or narrowly, by excluding some sources of income.

IF YOU CAN'T PAY

Many states have hardship provisions, but many judges are reluctant to deviate from the formula unless there's a very strong case. Possibilities may be:

- Extraordinary health expenses;
- Uninsured catastrophic losses;
- Child support paid for a child from a previous marriage.

Your ex-spouse may be willing to agree to reduce the amount of child support until you can return to a more stable place. You might also consider a trade, such as paying less child support for a while and paying more at a later date.

23 Most states allow for child support to be deducted directly from the pay check of a person who is failing to make payments.

BASIC GUIDELINES

Both parents' first and primary obligation is to support their children according to their ability to pay. The interest of children is usually the state's top priority. The purpose of child support is to ensure that the children will share in the standard of living of both parents regardless of where the children live or which parent cares for them.

22 Child support can't be permanently waived. The court always has the right to begin or adjust the amount.

OTHER FACTORS

The amount of child support typically increases based on the number of children to support. The percentage used in the court's formula varies from state to state. Some states also use a graduated or diminishing scale for all income beyond a certain amount. For example, all income above $100,000 might be subject to a different percentage from the first $100,000 of income.

In California, if a parent earns so much money that s/he could pay virtually any amount without hardship, the court may move away from the formula and focus instead on the reasonable needs of the child—a subjective concept both sides can argue.

THE EFFECT OF CUSTODY

The amount of time your children live with you generally affects the amount of child support you either pay or receive. This is called physical custody. This differs from legal custody in that legal custody governs who has the ability to make decisions concerning matters such as a child's medical care, religion, education, and welfare.

MORE TIME

The custodial parent is the one with primary physical custody. In other words, this is the one in whose house the child lives more than 50% of the time. In general, the more time a child lives with you, the more child support you will likely be entitled to receive.

EXPENSES GROW WITH THE KIDS

Keep in mind that raising children costs more as they get older and their universe expands. Their toys become more complicated (e.g., computers and cars). They need and want more clothes. They may go to private school where costs typically increase annually. As a single parent, you may need child care. There are after-school activities, entertainment, birthday parties, camp, music, tutoring, and uninsured health related expenses.

LESS TIME

Even if you aren't living with your children, you will still have parental responsibilities. A noncustodial parent (one who doesn't live with the children) is expected to contribute to the expenses of the children.

You might pay support to your ex-spouse in lump sums or send money on a regular schedule. You may also agree to pay certain expenses directly to the payee, such as the school, camp, or doctor. Making direct payments may give you more control over the money by ensuring that your payments are used for their intended purposes. If you pay your ex-spouse directly, you will probably not be able to control how the money is spent.

Some child support agreements include a mechanism for increasing support without returning to court. You may try to include a similar mechanism for decreasing child support in case of financial trouble.

◀ MORE CUSTODY, MORE SUPPORT

In general, if you're the one receiving child support, the more time a child lives in your home, the more support you will be entitled to receive.

EQUAL TIME

If a child lives in both homes, each of you will be responsible for expenses incurred while the child is with you. You still may want to share certain expenses, such as outfits for special occasions or education. Keep in mind, though, that even with 50/50 custody, the relative incomes of both parties may require one spouse to pay child support to the other.

Many experts advise that you try to work out the percentages of custody and payments yourselves. Leaving the court to decide who pays expenses may not lead to a result you or your ex-spouse will like.

BASIC GUIDELINES

You can agree to any amount you wish for child support. If, however, either party decides s/he no longer likes the agreement, the court has the authority to change it if it doesn't fall within the state's guidelines for child support.

HOW LONG DOES IT LAST?

Although you can agree otherwise, child support generally ends when your child reaches full legal age under your state's laws. Depending on the state, it could be age 18, 19, or 21. Certain situations could trigger an earlier end to child support. For example, your child could marry, enter the armed forces, or take a full-time job. If the child switches homes to live fulltime with the noncustodial parent, child support could end—or the payments could be reversed.

24 In some states, child support will continue even if the parent paying support dies.

SPOUSAL SUPPORT

*I*n a nutshell, the one who can afford to pay does, and the one who needs support receives it. The components of spousal support are the amount and the length of time support will be paid. If you settle out of court, almost any criteria can be used to determine support. Once in court, every state has their own guidelines. Some are discussed on these two pages.

WHAT IS SUPPORT?

Spousal support is a separate payment from child support. Its intent is to give one spouse a steady income to help defer his/her usual and unexpected costs of daily living. Of course, the laws differ from state to state, but there are some general concepts that carry through many states, such as:

No gender issue. The spouse receiving support can be either the man or the woman. Support is related to income capabilities, not gender.

Tax issues. Unless otherwise negotiated, spousal support payments are taxable as income to the one who receives it and tax deductible as an expense to the one who pays it. In other words, the recipient won't necessarily have the entire spousal support amount to spend and the one paying gets a tax break, unless otherwise negotiated.

Remarriage issue. Typically, when the recipient remarries, support payments stop, unless otherwise negotiated.

25 Negotiating disputes will save you from court orders that could end up pleasing neither you nor your ex-spouse.

MONETARY CONSIDERATIONS

Income. Is there sufficient money to enable both of you to enjoy the kind of lifestyle you once had, or are you both going to have to cut back?

Asset split. Since support is based largely on need, there may be little or no support if both parties are left with substantial assets after the divorce. The term "substantial" is subjective and it can be interpreted differently in different situations.

Independent income sources. Beyond the regular sources of income available for support, there is income that isn't part of the divorce negotiations, such as an asset brought to a marriage that remains the spouse's separate property. Even if an asset isn't subject to division in the divorce, its value might still affect the amount of support.

The effect of taxes. It's important to consider the net amount (after taxes) when calculating support payments.

TEMPORARY SUPPORT

Temporary spousal support is intended to help the spouse with less money to maintain the status quo during the separation period. In some states, the courts use guidelines to determine the appropriate amount of temporary support.

NON-MONETARY CONSIDERATIONS

Length of marriage. In general, the longer the marriage, the stronger the claim for support. In some states, a spouse married over ten years may be entitled to lifetime support.

Age. As a general rule, the younger you are, the more likely you will be able to work and increase your income over time. The closer you are to retirement, the more difficult it may be to earn income. A judge might make these presumptions when determining need and ability to pay.

Health. If one of you is ill or unable to work, that could affect the amount or length of support.

Education and job skills. A spouse's ability to become employed may affect the amount or length of support.

Parental time. A judge may decide that spousal support should be increased if child care responsibilities impose limits on job opportunities.

Job sacrifices during marriage. Support might increase in time or amount if one spouse sacrificed job possibilities so the other could take the work s/he wanted.

Fault. In states that consider fault, the reason for the divorce could affect the amount of support.

Past standard of living. In some states, maintaining "the lifestyle to which you have become accustomed" is an articulated goal. This doesn't mean, however, that the goal will be achieved.

TAXES

One of the important issues in divorce is the tax implications of your agreement. You need to understand what taxes are owed, what assets and income face tax consequences, what transfers will trigger new tax consequences, and how to protect yourself from IRS challenges.

FILING STATUS

The filing status you choose depends partly on your marital status on the last day of the year. Each has different consequences.

ARE YOU MARRIED?

For tax purposes, you're considered unmarried for the entire year if you've obtained a final decree of divorce or separate maintenance agreement by the last day of the year. Otherwise, you're considered married for the entire year, even if you're separated and live apart.

MARRIED FILING JOINTLY

If you're considered married, you and your spouse can file a joint return. A joint return reports your combined incomes and deductions and is signed by both you and your spouse.

Both of you are individually and jointly liable for any taxes, interest, or penalties due on a joint return. This means that you may be liable for the entire tax burden if your spouse is unable or unwilling to pay his/her share, even if you have no involvement with your spouse's business. This responsibility applies even after you are legally divorced and even if your divorce decree states that your former spouse will be responsible for any amounts due on past joint returns.

MARRIED FILING SEPARATELY

If you're considered married, you can opt for married filing separately. Some married couples file separate returns because both people want to be responsible for their own taxes, and not for each other's taxes.

In almost all cases, you will pay more combined tax with separate returns than you would pay with a joint return because the tax rate is higher. In addition, you can't take valuable tax credits for things such as child and dependent care, permanent disability, or the earned income tax credit available to certain low income individuals.

HEAD OF HOUSEHOLD

If you're considered unmarried, your filing status is either single or, if you meet certain requirements, head of household. You can file as head of household if you and your spouse live apart and have paid more than half the cost of keeping up the home that was the main home of your child or other dependent for more than six months of the year. This filing has the advantages of:

- A lower tax rate;
- A higher standard deduction;
- Potentially using dependency and other tax credits;
- Fewer restrictions on itemized deductions and personal exemptions than when married filing separately.

THINGS TO KNOW

Joint returns only. Some deductions can only be taken if you file a joint return. For example, this includes:

- Dependency exemption for a non-working spouse;
- Deduction for a spouse's contributions to an IRA.

Prepare estimates two ways. You may ask your accountant to prepare tax returns as a joint return and as separate returns (and head of household if you qualify). In this way, you will be able to determine which option gives you the best results for your circumstances.

Community property states. If you live in a community property state, you may be required to report community income earned or received by your spouse, even if you file separate returns.

Innocent spouses. Even if you file a joint return, you may not be liable for any additional taxes if your spouse makes errors or commits fraud without your knowledge (see pages 60-61 for more information).

WHO PAYS THE TAXES?

The income tax implications of support and property transfers are an important aspect of your agreement. You need to make sure you understand the tax consequences of decisions regarding child support, alimony (or spousal support), and the way assets are divided.

CHILD SUPPORT

The parent receiving support receives the money tax-free. The parent paying child support can't claim a deduction for the payment but is responsible for the taxes on that money—unless your agreement says otherwise.

SPOUSAL SUPPORT

Unlike child support, spousal support is taxed as income to the recipient and is deductible by the spouse who pays it.

PROPERTY TRANSFERS

In general,property transfers between spouses don't trigger a taxable gain or a taxable loss. Even if legally divorced, former spouses can transfer property tax free as long as the transfer is due to the divorce.

FAMILY SUPPORT

Some states may allow child and spousal support to be paid together as family support. For income tax purposes, family support (like spousal support) is taxed as income to the recipient and is deductible by the payer. In some cases, structuring support as family support can have advantages. For example, where the payer's tax bracket is higher than the recipient's tax bracket, family support provides an advantage to both parties.

---

26 Usually, your marital status as of Dec. 31st determines your filing status for the entire year.

SPOUSAL SUPPORT RECAPTURE

If your annual spousal support payments decrease by more than $15,000 or end during the first three years after your marriage ends, you may have to pay taxes on spousal support deducted in prior years. Support recapture should be considered in structuring a support arrangement. Be sure to discuss this issue with your divorce professional.

Form **4506**
(Rev. May 1997)
Department of the Treasury
Internal Revenue Service

Request for Copy or Transcript of Tax Form

► Read instructions before completing this form.

► Type or print clearly. Request may be rejected if the form is incomplete or illegible.

Note: *Do not use this form to get tax account information. Instead, see instructions below.*

OMB No. 1545-0429

1a Name shown on tax form. If a joint return, enter the name shown first.

2a If a joint return, spouse's name shown on tax form

1b First social security number on tax form or employer identification number (see instructions)

3 Current name, address (including apt. room, or suite no.), city, state, and ZIP code

2b Second social security number on tax form

4 Address, (including apt. room, or suite no.), city, state, and ZIP code shown on the last return filed if different from line 3

5 If copy of form or a tax return transcript is to be mailed to someone else, enter the third party's name and address

6 If we cannot find a record of your tax form and you want the payment refunded to the third party, check here ► ☐

7 If name in third party's records differs from line 1a above, enter that name here (see instructions)

8 Check only one box to show what you want. There is **no charge** for items 8a, b, and c:
  a ☐ Tax return transcript of Form 1040 series filed during the **current calendar year** and the 3 prior calendar years (see instructions)
  b ☐ Verification of nonfiling.
  c ☐ Form(s) W-2 information (see instructions).
  d ☐ Copy of tax form and all attachments (including Form(s) W-2, schedules, or other forms). **The charge is $23 for each period requested.**
  Note: *If these copies must be certified for court or administrative proceedings, see instructions and check here* ► ☐

9 If this request is to meet a requirement of one of the following, check all boxes that apply.
  ☐ Small Business Administration   ☐ Department of Education   ☐ Department of Veterans Affairs

10 Tax form number (Form 1040, 1040A, 941, etc.)

Tax

THINGS TO KNOW

- If you live in a community property state and you and your spouse file separate returns, you may each be responsible for reporting half of any community income. Your state law determines whether income is separate or community income.

- Taxable spousal support is treated as compensation for purposes of the IRA contribution and deduction limits. This means you can make a tax deductible IRA contribution even if you don't work.

IF YOU NEED ▲ PAST TAX RECORDS

You can contact the IRS and ask for Form 4506. By signing and returning it to the IRS, you will give them the proof they need to send you all signed copies. Note that you won't receive any tax forms that aren't signed by you, even if signed by your spouse.

GET IT IN WRITING ▼

It's important to get your agreement in writing. Spousal support is only tax deductible if it's based on a final divorce decree or separate maintenance agreement signed by both parties.

57

DEDUCTIONS, CREDITS, AND EXEMPTIONS

There are a number of ways you may be able to reduce taxes, depending on your arrangement with your spouse.

ITEMIZED DEDUCTIONS

Medical expenses. In most cases, a child's medical expenses can be taken as a medical deduction by both parents for purposes of the medical expense deduction.

Legal fees. Generally, you can't deduct legal fees and court costs associated with divorce. You may, however, be able to deduct legal fees for tax advice connected to your divorce, and legal fees connected to the spousal support you report as taxable income. You may also be able to deduct fees to appraisers, actuaries, and other professionals who help you determine your taxes or help you obtain spousal support.

TAX BREAKS BASED ON DEPENDENTS

Dependent exemptions. Generally, the parent with more physical custody is allowed to claim the exemption. The custodial parent can, however, sign a dependency release (Form 8832) agreeing not to claim the exemption for the child so that the non-custodial parent can take it with his/her return. An exemption can be released for a year, a specified number of years or for all future years.

Child tax credit. You may be eligible for a tax credit that directly reduces your taxes (up to $500 for each child under age 17). Generally, whoever has the dependent exemption is also entitled to the child credit. The credit begins to phase out once your income is over $110,000 (for joint filers) and $75,000 for single taxpayers.

Additional child tax credit. If you have three or more children, you may be entitled to a refund even if you don't pay any tax. Check with a tax professional.

EARNED INCOME TAX CREDIT

In general, relatively low income earners may be entitled to a tax credit that reduces the amount of tax owed (if any) to offset some of their living expenses and Social Security taxes.

This credit isn't available to people who file a married filing separate return. There are a number of specific criteria you must meet to be eligible. For example, you must earn less than $10,200 (as of 1999) if you have no children, and less than $26,928 if you have one qualifying child, or less than $30,580 if you have more than one qualifying child. Consult a tax professional concerning the definitions of a qualifying child and about the other specific criteria to see whether you qualify.

27 You can decide which spouse will claim a child as a tax exemption, regardless of custody.

OTHER ISSUES TO CONSIDER

Tax withholding and estimated payments. When you become divorced or spearated you may have to file a new W4 to avoid witholding too little on your pay checks. If you receive alimony you may have to make estimated tax payments to cover the extra income.
Sales of property. If you sell property that's owned jointly you must report your share of the gain or loss on your tax return in the year of sale. This is true even if you're no longer legally married.

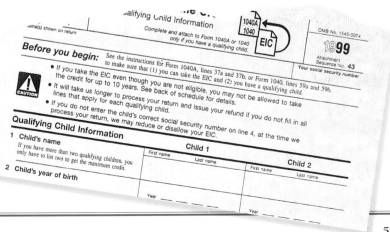

EDUCATION TAX BREAKS

Whether or not you are the parent with
primary custody, if you're paying
tuition for a child, you may be entitled to
one or both of the tuition tax breaks
available to Americans. Ask your child's
college financial aid office for the form you
will need to complete.

WHO IS ELIGIBLE
To be eligible, a student must:
- Be enrolled at least half-time
  in an eligible program at an
  eligible school;
- Be a freshman or sophomore
  in college;
- Not have been convicted of a
  felony drug offense before the
  end of the tax year in which
  the school year ends.

WHO CAN USE EDUCATION CREDITS

To be eligible, you must:
- File a tax return;
- Owe taxes (not be receiving a refund);
- Claim the student as your dependent
  on the tax return (unless the student
  is you or your spouse);
- (Only for the Hope Scholarship) owe
  less in taxes than the maximum credit
  available to you.

LIFETIME LEARNING TAX CREDIT
This is a tax credit for:
- Up to $1,000 a year (until Jan. 1,
  2003, then $2,000 per year after);
- Each family (not each student);
- An unlimited number of years.
You claim 20% of up to $5,000 of
paid eligible expenses (20% of
$10,000 after Jan.1, 2003). There's
no refund if the credit is larger than
the amount of tax you owe.

HOPE SCHOLARSHIP
Scholarship is a misleading name.
This is actually a tax credit for:
- Up to $1,500 a year per eligible
  college student;
- No more than two tax years.
You claim up to 100% of the first
$1,000 of eligible expenses and 50%
of the next $1,000 (which makes a
maximum of $1,500). You don't get
a refund if the credit is larger than
the tax you owe.

USING THE CREDITS

To avoid a situation where no one can use the education credits, some experts suggest one of these:

- The spouse with the dependent exemption waives it and lets the spouse paying tuition take it;
- The spouse with custody gets an increase in spousal support (and a deduction elsewhere), pays the tuition and takes the credit;
- Gift tuition to the child and the gifting parent takes the tax credit.

NO LIMIT ▼

There's no total dollar limit per family for the education tax credits. So if you have three kids in college, you could potentially have three $1,500 tax credits.

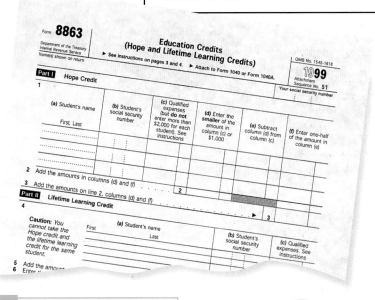

Form **8863**						
Department of the Treasury Internal Revenue Service	**Education Credits (Hope and Lifetime Learning Credits)** ► See instructions on pages 3 and 4. ► Attach to Form 1040 or Form 1040A.				OMB No. 1545-1618	
Name(s) shown on return					**1999** Attachment Sequence No. **51**	
					Your social security number	

Part I Hope Credit

1	(a) Student's name First, Last	(b) Student's social security number	(c) Qualified expenses (but **do not** enter more than $2,000 for each student. See instructions	(d) Enter the **smaller** of the amount in column (c) or $1,000	(e) Subtract column (d) from column (c)	(f) Enter one-half of the amount in column (e)

2 Add the amounts in columns (d) and (f) . . . . | | **2** | |

3 Add the amounts on line 2, columns (d) and (f) . . . . ► | **3** |

Part II Lifetime Learning Credit

4

Caution: You cannot take the Hope credit and the lifetime learning credit for the same student.

	(a) Student's name First Last	(b) Student's social security number	(c) Qualified expenses. See instructions

5 Add the amounts
6 Enter t...

28 If you pay tuition but your spouse claims the student as a dependent, no one will get the tax credit.

THE INNOCENT SPOUSE RULE

This IRS rule can release people who've filed joint returns from tax liabilities created by their spouse if they meet certain stringent criteria. It's not, however, a guarantee.

HOW IT WORKS

Decisions are made on a case by case basis, and the burden is on the spouse seeking relief.

To qualify, the IRS says the following criteria must be met:

- You filed a joint return for the tax year in question;
- There was a misrepresentation of at least $500 of income, deductions, or credits;
- The spouse seeking relief establishes that when s/he signed the return s/he didn't know—and had no reason to know—about the underreporting of the taxes.

If all criteria are met, the spouse seeking relief may be released from liability for any tax, interest, and penalties related to the underreporting of the taxes.

There have also been cases where the court has determined that the spouse's lack of ability to understand the financial decisions releases him or her from liability. Other cases have raised the issue of whether or not the spouse received any benefit from the misrepresentation made by the other spouse.

If you think this rule applies to you, consult an attorney. This area is particularly complicated.

INNOCENT SPOUSE TEST RULING

A recent United States Court of Appeals decision held that a woman didn't automatically lose out on innocent spouse relief simply because she knew her ex-husband had invested in a tax shelter and received tax deductions that were later disallowed by the IRS. The Court stated that the test should include the question of whether the spouse had the sophisticated financial insight to understand the tax shelter.

29 You must file for relief within two years from the time the IRS first tried to collect the tax from you.

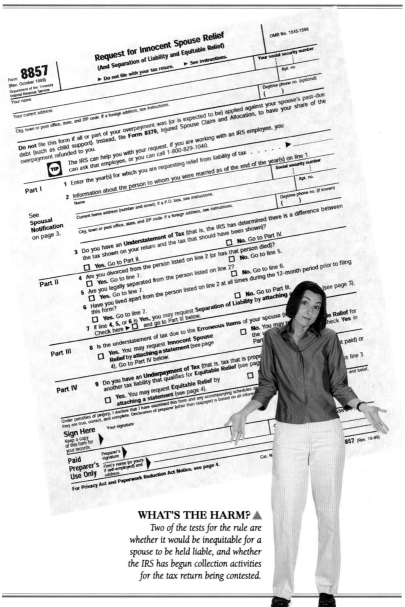

Form 8857 (Rev. October 1999)
Department of the Treasury
Internal Revenue Service

Request for Innocent Spouse Relief
(And Separation of Liability and Equitable Relief)
▶ See instructions.
▶ Do not file with your tax return.

OMB No. 1545-1596

Your name

Your social security number

Your current address

Apt. no.

City, town or post office, state, and ZIP code. If a foreign address, see instructions.

Daytime phone no. (optional)
( )

Do not file this form if all or part of your overpayment was (or is expected to be) applied against your spouse's past-due debt (such as child support). Instead, file **Form 8379**, Injured Spouse Claim and Allocation, to have your share of the overpayment refunded to you.

(TIP) The IRS can help you with your request. If you are working with an IRS employee, you can ask that employee, or you can call 1-800-829-1040. ▶

Part I

1 Enter the year(s) for which you are requesting relief from liability of tax . . . . . ▶

2 Information about the person to whom you were married as of the end of the year(s) on line 1.

Name

Social security number

Current home address (number and street). If a P.O. box, see instructions.

Apt. no.

City, town or post office, state, and ZIP code. If a foreign address, see instructions.

Daytime phone no. (if known)
( )

See **Spousal Notification** on page 3.

Part II

3 Do you have an **Understatement of Tax** (that is, the IRS has determined there is a difference between the tax shown on your return and the tax that should have been shown)?
☐ **Yes.** Go to Part II. ☐ **No.** Go to Part IV.

4 Are you divorced from the person listed on line 2 (or has that person died)?
☐ **Yes.** Go to line 7. ☐ **No.** Go to line 5.

5 Are you legally separated from the person listed on line 2?
☐ **Yes.** Go to line 7. ☐ **No.** Go to line 6.

6 Have you lived apart from the person listed on line 2 at all times during the 12-month period prior to filing this form?
☐ **Yes.** Go to line 7. ☐ **No.** Go to Part III.

7 If line **4, 5, or 6** is Yes, you may request **Separation of Liability** by attaching a (see page 3).
Check here ▶ ☐ and go to Part III below.

Part III

8 Is the understatement of tax due to the **Erroneous Items** of your spouse (s
☐ **Yes.** You may request **Innocent Spouse**
Relief by attaching a statement (see page 4). Go to Part IV below.
☐ **No.** You may re

Part IV

9 Do you have an **Underpayment of Tax** (that is, tax that is prope
another tax liability that qualifies for **Equitable Relief** (see pag
☐ **Yes.** You may request **Equitable Relief** by attaching a statement (see page 4).

Under penalties of perjury, I declare that I have examined this form and any accompanying schedules a
they are true, correct, and complete. Declaration of preparer (other than taxpayer) is based on all inform

Sign Here
Keep a copy
of this form for
your records.

Your signature ▶

Paid Preparer's Use Only
Preparer's signature ▶
Firm's name (or yours if self-employed) and address

For Privacy Act and Paperwork Reduction Act Notice, see page 4.

Cat. N

857 (Rev. 10-99)

WHAT'S THE HARM? ▲

Two of the tests for the rule are whether it would be inequitable for a spouse to be held liable, and whether the IRS has begun collection activities for the tax return being contested.

STATE-BY-STATE OVERVIEWS

Since divorce laws differ in every state, this chapter offers some general guidelines covering property and support. Be sure to check with a legal advisor in your state to verify the information.

PROPERTY DIVISION

STATE	COMMUNITY PROPERTY	ONLY MARITAL DIVIDED	STATUTORY LIST OF FACTORS	NONMONETARY CONTRIBUTIONS	ECONOMIC MISCONDUCT	CONTRIBUTION TO EDUCATION
ALABAMA		X		X		X
ALASKA			X	X	X	X
ARIZONA	X				X	X
ARKANSAS		X	X	X		
CALIFORNIA	X		X	X	X	X
COLORADO		X	X	X	X	
CONNECTICUT			X	X	X	X
DELAWARE			X	X	X	
DIST. OF COL.		X	X	X	X	
FLORIDA		X	X	X	X	X
GEORGIA		X				
HAWAII			X	X	X	
IDAHO	X		X			
ILLINOIS		X	X	X	X	
INDIANA		X	X	X	X	X
IOWA			X	X	X	X
KANSAS			X		X	
KENTUCKY		X	X	X	X	X

STATE	COMMUNITY PROPERTY	ONLY MARITAL DIVIDED	STATUTORY LIST OF FACTORS	NONMONETARY CONTRIBUTIONS	ECONOMIC MISCONDUCT	CONTRIBUTION TO EDUCATION
LOUISIANA	X					
MAINE		X	X	X	X	
MARYLAND		X	X	X	X	
MASSACHUSETTS			X	X	X	X
MICHIGAN		X		X	X	X
MINNESOTA		X	X	X	X	
MISSISSIPPI		X		X	X	X
MISSOURI		X	X	X	X	X
MONTANA			X	X	X	
NEBRASKA		X		X		
NEVADA	X	X		X	X	X
NEW HAMPSHIRE			X	X	X	X
NEW JERSEY		X	X	X	X	X
NEW MEXICO	X					
NEW YORK		X	X	X	X	X
NORTH CAROLINA		X	X	X	X	X
NORTH DAKOTA				X	X	X
OHIO		X	X	X	X	X
OKLAHOMA		X		X	X	
OREGON				X	X	X
PENNSYLVANIA		X	X	X	X	X
RHODE ISLAND		X	X	X	X	X
SOUTH CAROLINA		X	X	X	X	X
SOUTH DAKOTA				X	X	
TENNESSEE		X	X	X	X	X
TEXAS	X				X	
UTAH					X	
VERMONT			X	X	X	X
VIRGINIA		X	X	X	X	
WASHINGTON	X		X			
WEST VIRGINIA		X	X	X	X	X
WISCONSIN	X	X	X	X	X	X
WYOMING		X	X	X[1]		

1. By case law.
Source: Reprinted by permission of the American Bar Association

CHILD SUPPORT GUIDELINES BY STATE
TABLES SUMMARIZING THE LAW IN THE FIFTY STATES

STATE	INCOME SHARE	% OF INCOME	MEDICAL ADD ON	CHILDCARE ADD ON	COLLEGE SUPPORT
ALABAMA	X		X	X	X
ALASKA		X	X		
ARIZONA	X		X	X	
ARKANSAS		X			
CALIFORNIA	X		X	X	
COLORADO	X		X	X	
CONNECTICUT	X				
DELAWARE			X	X	
DIST. OF COL.		X	X	X	X
FLORIDA	X		X	X	
GEORGIA		X	X	X	
HAWAII		X		X	X
IDAHO	X		X	X	
ILLINOIS		X			X
INDIANA	X		X	X	X
IOWA		X			X
KANSAS	X		X	X	
KENTUCKY	X		X	X	
LOUISIANA	X		X	X	
MAINE	X		X	X	
MARYLAND	X		X	X	
MASSACHUSETTS		X	X	X	X
MICHIGAN	X		X	X	X
MINNESOTA		X		X	
MISSISSIPPI		X			
MISSOURI	X		X	X	X
MONTANA			X	X	
NEBRASKA	X			X	
NEVADA		X	X		

STATE	INCOME SHARE	% OF INCOME	MEDICAL ADD ON	CHILDCARE ADD ON	COLLEGE SUPPORT[2]
NEW HAMPSHIRE		X			X
NEW JERSEY	X		X	X	X
NEW MEXICO	X		X	X	
NEW YORK	X		X	X	X
NORTH CAROLINA	X		X	X	
NORTH DAKOTA		X		X	
OHIO	X			X	
OKLAHOMA	X		X	X	
OREGON	X		X	X	X
PENNSYLVANIA	X		X	X	
RHODE ISLAND	X			X	
SOUTH CAROLINA	X		X	X	X
SOUTH DAKOTA	X	X	X	X	
TENNESSEE		X			X
TEXAS		X	X		
UTAH	X		X	X	
VERMONT	X		X	X	
VIRGINIA	X		X	X	
WASHINGTON	X		X	X	X
WEST VIRGINIA	X		X	X	
WISCONSIN		X	X		
WYOMING	X	X	X[1]	X	

All 54 U.S. jurisdictions have enacted UIFSA as of Spring 1998.

1. Any other necessary expenses of child within court's discretion.

2. Most states will enforce an agreement of the parties.

Source: Reprinted by permission of the American Bar Association.

ALIMONY/SPOUSAL SUPPORT FACTORS

STATE	STATUTORY LIST	MARITAL FAULT NOT CONSIDERED	MARITAL FAULT RELEVANT	STANDARD OF LIVING	STATUS AS CUSTODIAL PARENT
ALABAMA			X	X	
ALASKA	X	X		X	X
ARIZONA	X	X		X	X
ARKANSAS		X			
CALIFORNIA	X	X		X	
COLORADO	X	X		X	X
CONNECTICUT	X		X	X	X
DELAWARE	X	X		X	X
DIST. OF COL.			X	X	
FLORIDA	X		X	X	
GEORGIA	X		X	X	
HAWAII	X	X		X	X
IDAHO	X		X		
ILLINOIS	X	X		X	X
INDIANA	X	X		X	X
IOWA	X	X		X	X
KANSAS		X			
KENTUCKY	X		X[1]	X	
LOUISIANA	X		X		X
MAINE	X	X			
MARYLAND	X		X	X	
MASSACHUSETTS	X		X	X	
MICHIGAN			X	X	
MINNESOTA	X	X		X	X
MISSISSIPPI			X		
MISSOURI	X		X	X	X
MONTANA	X	X		X	X
NEBRASKA	X	X		X	X

STATE	STATUTORY LIST	MARITAL FAULT NOT CONSIDERED	MARITAL FAULT RELEVANT	STANDARD OF LIVING	STATUS AS CUSTODIAL PARENT
NEVADA			X	X	X
NEW HAMPSHIRE	X		X	X	X
NEW JERSEY	X		X	X	X
NEW MEXICO	X	X		X	
NEW YORK	X		X	X	X
NORTH CAROLINA	X		X	X	
NORTH DAKOTA			X	X	
OHIO	X	X			
OKLAHOMA		X		X	X
OREGON	X	X		X	X
PENNSYLVANIA	X		X	X	
RHODE ISLAND	X		X	X	X
SOUTH CAROLINA	X		X	X	X
SOUTH DAKOTA			X	X	
TENNESSEE	X		X	X	X
TEXAS	X		X	X	X
UTAH	X		X	X	
VERMONT	X	X		X	X
VIRGINIA	X		X	X	
WASHINGTON	X	X		X	
WEST VIRGINIA	X		X		X
WISCONSIN	X	X		X	X
WYOMING			X		

1. Only fault on the part of the party seeking alimony.

Source: Reprinted by permission of the American Bar Association

INDEX

ACKNOWLEDGMENTS

AUTHORS' ACKNOWLEDGMENTS

The production of this book has relied on the skills of many people. Most of all, it is due to the generous and skilled attention of Stephanie Blum. Stephanie was called upon with very short notice to provide not just information for this book, but truly useful information that anyone can understand. Despite a very busy practice, she was remarkably giving of her time, knowledge, and enthusiasm. Stephanie and Marc also owe a tremendous debt of gratitude to Stuart Allen who, on even shorter notice, added to his already long hours to provide expert clarifications, fine tuning, and especially fine writing. This book was improved immeasurably—and Stephanie's and Marc's lives were made immeasurably easier— by Stuart's outstanding skill, energy, and thoughtfulness. We would also like to thank Dwight Harris, pension consultant in Los Angeles, for his excellent help with retirement issues. We would like to mention our editors at Dorling Kindersley for their support and efforts. Stephanie wishes to give special thanks to Bob Nachshin and Scott Weston for providing her the opportunity to pursue her professional goals and the support and guidance necessary to achieve them. Marc wishes to dedicate this book to Zachary Robinson for his great patience and support when it was most needed, and to Bert and Phoebe Robinson for the unquestioned support they provided in so many ways whenever it was asked.

PUBLISHER'S ACKNOWLEDGMENTS

Dorling Kindersley would like to thank everyone who generously lent props for the photo shoots, and the following for their help and participation:

Editorial Stephanie Rubenstein; **Design and Layout** Jill Dupont; **Consultants** Nick Clemente; Skeeter; **Indexer** Rachel Rice; **Proofreader** Stephanie Rubenstein; **Photography** Anthony Nex; **Photographers' assistants** Damon Dulas; **Models** Stephanie Rose; Anthony Nex; Kristine Nex; **Picture researcher** Mark Dennis; Sam Ruston; **Content Consultant** Stuart D. Allen, CPA/ABV is a senior member in the firm of Cohen, Miskei & Mowrey, LLP, located in Encino, California. Mr. Allen has specialized in forensic accounting, litigation consulting, business valuation, and expert testimony services for over ten years. The majority of Mr. Allen's practice is devoted to the area of family law.

Special thanks to Teresa Clavasquin for her generous support and assistance.

AUTHORS' BIOGRAPHIES

Stephanie I. Blum is a family law attorney practicing with the law firm of Nachshin & Weston, LLP in Los Angeles, California. She obtained her undergraduate degree from Cornell University in 1987. After a brief stint in the wire business in New York City, Stephanie went back to school and obtained her law degree from the University of Southern California. Stephanie's other credits include co-authoring an article in California Lawyer on prenuptual agreements.

Marc Robinson is co-founder of Internet-based moneytours.com, a personal finance resource for corporations, universities, credit unions, and other institutions interested in helping their constituents make intelligent decisions about their financial lives. He wrote the original The Wall Street Journal Guide to Understanding Money and Markets, created The Wall Street Journal Guide to Understanding Personal Finance, co-published a personal finance series with Time Life Books, and wrote a children's book about onomateopia in different languages. In his two decades in the financial services industry, Marc has provided marketing consulting to many top Wall Street firms. He is admitted to practice law in New York State.